AF335630

A

KISS

For People Who Believe In Love

by

JERRY SCHURR

and illustrated by

GAIL CHRISTOPHERSON-SCHURR

Goode Publishing Co.

4005 Manzanita Avenue, #6B
Carmichael, California 95608
(916) 488-6690

Library of Congress Catalog Card Number: 92-74077

Schurr, Jerry.
    A Kiss, For People Who Believe In Love.

ISBN 1-882303-00-8

PREFACE

The author is many things. He is a writer. He is a poet. He shares the ownership of a real estate business with his wife, Gail Christopherson-Schurr. It is a seven-day-per-week business requiring schedules which are nonexistent and flexibility which is uncommon.

Gail, is an accountant, a client entertainer, a home decorator, an executive secretary, a stepmother to Jerry's three daughters from a former marriage, a mother to their son, age four, and not least—a gifted, graphic artist. Among other things, she painted the late Sammy Davis, Jr.'s favorite portrait painting and created the illustrations in this book. She is his incredible wife, lover and soul mate.

The inspiration for these poems, for the most part, is her fault. The blame lies with her. If you should find this collection of romantic poems, toasts and bouquet notes having added some value to your love life– then blame it on her! Write her a letter because–after all—it's her fault!

ORDER TODAY

A KISS

For People Who Believe In Love

When you order:	The price is:
1 – 3	$16.50 Each
4 – 9	$13.20 Each
10 – 24	$11.58 Each

✳ Add local tax (your area) + shipping fee ($2.50 each)
In California for 1 book the total is $20.36 ($16.50 + $1.36 tax + $2.50).
✳ Note: Shipping fee for ten or more books is $2.00 each.

Thank you for "believing in love."

ALWAYS

Check your local bookstores first and you will avoid shipping costs.

Ask for ISBN #1-882303-00-8

- -

GOODE PUBLISHING CO.   (916) 488-6690
4005 Manzanita Ave., #6B, Carmichael, CA 95608

- -

Quantity   __________   SEND TO:______________________
    x Price   __________
Subtotal   __________   Address ________________________
    x Tax Rate   __________   City____________________________
Subtotal   __________
    + Shipping Costs __________   State______________ Zip__________

    TOTAL   __________   **AS A GIFT**

                               FROM:_________________________

Enclose check or money order
made payable to: Address________________________

                               City____________________________
GOODE PUBLISHING CO.
                               State______________ Zip__________

MESSAGE: ____
____

PLEASE PHOTOCOPY THIS ORDER FORM, COMPLETE AND RETURN.

INDEX

How can there be an index to love? Well, we'll try.

INTRODUCTION	6
LOVE IS WHAT MATTERS	7
A KISS	9
LOOKING FOR LOVE	11
TOGETHER	13
SOUL RAPTURE	15
WHEN I THINK ABOUT HER	17
TOASTS FOR A ROMANTIC EVENING	19
MY LOVE IS YOURS	21
TOASTS FOR A GLOOMY AFTERNOON	23
LOVE FALLING MY WAY	25
ROMANTIC TOASTS TO CELEBRATE EVENTS	27
OUR LOVE IS MORE THAN TWO	29
LOYALTY	32
MARRY	36
ROMANTIC BOUQUET NOTES	39
LONGEVITY	42
ELEGANT LOVE	46
FINAL THOUGHTS	48

INTRODUCTION

*T*his collection of poems and "toasts to romantic evenings out"—are *real—my love for Gail—the lady in my universe! There's no steamy, sensual, ribaldry tales here—just real love between two people who know each other as the soul mate of the other.*

Real, then as our love in time unfolds. We hope you enjoy walking in the footpaths of our roads.

These poems require no knowledge of us as lovers. They speak honestly for themselves from everyday living.

However, for those of you who would like a peek behind the scenes, we will provide a short narrative about our beginnings and a few paragraphs about the circumstances behind each poem prior to your reading them. It will probably be more fun to simply read each poem without any of the embellishment.

by Jerry Schurr, Author

LOVE IS WHAT MATTERS

*I*n a marriage relationship words and actions between partners build bonding and lasting ties or they slowly chip away the infrastructure. Time is the test. We can only know our true selves over time. Our partners (spouses) gain or lose from our abilities to understand the real world—which is always changing—and we, ourselves, are always changing and growing.

Love is a challenge—a delight—a necessity—a belief. It's simple and absolutely worthwhile. As long as you both can share and support each other's beliefs—through tough times your love will last. Love is more than forbearance—it is joy in sharing your lives together—and knowing that the two of you is all that counts.

In the final analysis, love is what matters. From it springs all good activities that man strives for—justice, peace, better living conditions, sharing and enduring for humanity's sake. The joy of living, laughing and accepting one's own frailties—keeping life in perspective—and just doing the best we can with our circumstances— we do it all for love.

Please, now, don't be fooled by the word, love. And, please, don't try to fool anyone else by the use of it. Too many people abuse the word and are really looking out for their own selfish interests—hiding behind it and manipulating others for their own gains. I can't imagine anyone who has not experienced false love. So horrible is its experience that it remains an anger in us, so that we will try to not experience its pain again.

True love by its virtues has always seemed best expressed to me from a passage in the Bible. First Corinthians, Thirteen, verses four through seven read, "Love is patient and kind; it is not jealous or conceited or proud; love is not ill-mannered or selfish or irritable; love does not keep a record of wrongs; love is not happy with evil, but is happy with the truth. Love never gives up; and its faith, hope and patience never fail."

A KISS

Background

It seems to me that love always begins with this—a kiss. Oh, sure, there are always imaginings and fantasizings; hopings and mopings; wonderings and longings.

There may even be conversations and forays; don't forget dances and sly or intent glances—some will even say trances.

The truth, perceived from my short experience with it, is that nothing truly substantial begins until—the kiss.

Then, WATCH OUT!

A KISS

A kiss

Is the bending

Of two temples near,

To combine two souls

Into one atmosphere,

Resulting in the emotion

Of Love so dear.

end.

© 1986

LOOKING FOR LOVE

Background

We all do it. You may say, "I don't need it." "It's too much trouble." "I don't have time for it." "There's no Mr. or Ms. Right for me." Whatever you say now won't last. There will be some times, some moments in your life when the need will suddenly become paramount in your life.

There's nothing wrong with it. Feeling needed, appreciated and sharing your special feelings and talents with someone who cares is wonderful. God intended it to be that way. Once you find your "someone," you'll never want to let them go.

There's no magical way to find your "someone special" to love. It usually catches us off-guard when we're least expecting it. We're disarmed by it. And functioning in a normal manner seems to be a total struggle, almost impossible.

We all have our stories and memories that are near and dear to our hearts. Oftentimes it's those memories that keep us going, living for more moments in time that will make life worth living.

When I met Gail, writing love poems was not on my mind. Writing was and finding someone who understood that 'drive' to be artistic and not being offended by it was of vital importance.

This poem, then, is Gail's fault (as I've stated before). Hopefully it will reflect some of your own feelings and experiences.

Remember that genuine love is totally worthwhile.

LOOKING FOR LOVE

I know there must be
Someone
Somewhere
Looking for me.
Someone who seeks
To blend their soul
With mine
In harmony.

But,
Why does it seem
So hard
To find my dream
To find a soul to lean on
To put my soul in song?

I've given myself
Behind closed doors
Listened to bores
Hoped
For a wealthy store
Of a soul's hidden
Treasure
A common substance
I could
Measure.

These days of looking
Are so dull
Empty
Confusing.
My heart aches
For God's sake.

I'm tired of gray days
The daily parades
Of meaningless escapades.
Where
Are the sun's rays
Shining
On solid human clay?

A substance
With resonance
Caring
Only
For my innocence
Sharing
Only
Their naturalness;

A commonness
In spirit
Is what I seek
To share
Sunrises
Surprises
Kisses
Blisses
Each day's joy
A true story
Of love
Between you and me.

Oh, God, please let it be.

© 1986

TOGETHER

Background

Our meeting was the most unlikely of situations. It is one of those things that doesn't make sense and can only be answered out of the realization of our NEEDS—and somehow sensing that we should be together (let me add, forever).

It was the Christmas season when we met. I was being helpful. Her Christmas tree lights wouldn't work. She offered me a homemade dinner for my troubles. I accepted. At dinner's end she asked me if there was anything else she could do for me for my repair work. "Never ask a man a question like that!" And so, I said, "How about a kiss?"

And, as you know, "It all begins with a kiss."

TOGETHER

Together
Alone
Side by side.

No longer
Needing
To hide.

Inner feelings
From the world
Outside.

No longer
Playing
Mature
Cool
Beautiful
Macho
Institutional.

No longer
Being
Leader
Follower
Servant
Used
Abused
First or
Second class.

No longer
Needing
Artificial supports
Cars
Clothes
Drinks
Needing
Nothing
That distorts.

But, being
Myself
Alone
With you.

Confiding
In you
Disappointments
Joys
Aspirations
Real situations.

Accepting
You
Being real
With me.

The two of us
Together
Reaching out
Letting love start.

Feeling
Each other's
Souls
Hands
Hearts
Inner parts.

Sharing
The richness of
Humanity
Supporting
Eternity.

Being
A voice
A movement
An energy
Together
Creating
A synergy.

A softness
Naturalness
Filling in
The emptiness.

Rekindling
Hope
Kindness
Happiness
Loftiness.

Celebrating
You
Celebrating
Me.

Making
Our lives
Together
A treasury.

© 1986

SOUL RAPTURE

Background

This was my second poem to Gail. Our first months together were exciting and wonderful. They were full of fun and laughter. They also had their moments of concern—wondering if—I was real—if she was real. Would our meeting of chance and circumstance last? Was it euphoria or a madness that adults travel through? I knew and felt and believed that love was in our hearts. It was simply too late for me, anyway. And so, this is what I said:

SOUL RAPTURE

The air
Is rich and pure and rare.
The stars are gossiping.
They shimmer and flare.
I think they stare!
There is a new love they share.

Born out of blue moods,
Blue moons,
Empty noons.
Tempered by hollow feuds,
Shallow souls,
Dismal goals.

Our eyes crystallize
Into joys and sighs
Sharing
Life's true highs.
Twirling, swirling, soaring,
Making souls fly.
Quelling,
Submerging sad songs,
Former wrongs.

Your smile,
My smile–
We race
Into each other's face,
Embrace–

Lifting spirits,
Restoring faith.

Love grows.
Our souls know
Life is building,
Dreams fulfilling.
The world is real again.

© 1986

WHEN I THINK ABOUT HER

Background

We took the greatest chance! There was no good reason that our love or marriage would work. Looking back, I suppose it was out of enormous and incredible NEED to find someone who would support our creative desires—to express ourselves. And HOPE that others would see in us something special enough to purchase from us because what we painted and/or wrote struck the high, pure note of truth in themselves. And that what they found in us would inspire them to accept themselves with happiness and would make them strive to be more than they were before they met us.

Sounds corny, doesn't it. True artists, real artists—whose purpose is purely to pour out their souls—this is how we feel—want to inspire, entertain, create beauty, even solve invisible and mysterious problems. Yes, I think scientists are artists—possibly even plumbers—anyone who takes their work seriously. Recognition, for the talent God bestowed upon you, is what we all strive for—we are tormented about leaving mankind something which pours out of the soul of us as God planted the seed within us.

There was something inside of me that I had to tell Gail about. These feelings I felt about her as our days together unfolded. It was as if she had put me in her trance and I had welcomed it wholeheartedly. I was absolutely amazed at my great, good fortune in finding her. This poem is her in all her wonderful ways and she is even more than this today (but, please, don't tell her).

WHEN I THINK ABOUT HER

When I
Think about
Her

I feel
Amused.
Her smile
Her laugh
So genuine,
Light and hearty
Makes me laugh

Forget
Pressures,
Deadlines,
Overtime;
Look forward
To evening time

When I
Think about
Her

Voice
Melodious
And sensuous
Interrupts
My thoughts
Connects
My heart
And ear
Makes my
Breathing
Stop

When I
Think about
Her

Sadness
Brings me
Tears
And I've
Known her
Less than
A year

When I
Think about
Her

Gentle ways
Graceful
Flowing
In my mind.
Timeless days
Pass her way.
I wish she
Would stay.

When I
Think about
Her

Mind
Clear and sharp
Kind
Full of joy
Forgiving
Needing no glory
Having her own story
Living simply
Seeking her destiny
Easily

When I
Think about
Her

Attractiveness
Neat and clean
Orderly
Full of self-pride
A joy
To be beside

Her hand
In mine
Transferring
Spirit
Reminiscent
Of a soul
Innocent
Radiant

Filling me
With
Love,
Love.
Love
It's all
I can
Think of.

© 1986

TOASTS FOR A ROMANTIC
EVENING

Background

It was by accident, of course,—and a little bit of the romanticist in me—that I began making toasts for every round of brandy manhattans-on-the-rocks or first glass of wine that we drank together. After busy and difficult days, weeks and months—and even years—as it has turned out, there is a renewal, a rejoicing, a camaraderie and for us—a binding and blending of our souls together just from this use of—TOASTS!

We believe that you should try a few of these between yourselves to see if they lengthen the evening and bring your feelings in touch with one another together.

I wish we could remember all of them. However, this book is a recent inspiration and many eons have passed before this time.

TOASTS FOR A ROMANTIC EVENING

Toast No. 1.
"Thank you for sharing your life with me."

Toast No. 2.
"When I think of you, I think of love."

Toast No. 3.
"Thank you for making my life worthwhile."

Toast No. 4.
"There is no joy in life without you."

Toast No. 5.
"Joy of Joys you are to me. Night and Day and in every way."

Toast No. 6.
"You look and smell absolutely irresistible. I think
it's time to take you home."

Toast No. 7.
"Being with you fills my whole life with happiness."

Toast No. 8.
"It's a privilege to be with a woman who is
so beautiful."

Toast No. 9.
"I'm spellbound by your beauty."

Toast No. 10.
"Being able to share tonight with you makes a difficult week easy."

MY LOVE IS YOURS

Background

*I*n the beginning love is uncertain. It's a fragile thing and can be
especially unpredictable if you're not aware of the background feelings
and experience of your mate.

*This poem was written to Gail during one of those moments in which she
had some feelings that I might not have been as in love with her as I was. It
was, of course, bewildering to me because I knew without any doubts,
whatsoever, that we were going to be bound together through eternity.*

MY LOVE IS YOURS

Gail,
I can't
Love
You
More
Than
I do
It's true

No Love
Exists
More
Than
This
Experience
I Share
With
You

It
Can't
Be lost
In
Darkness
Storm
Or frost
At any cost

My Love
Is yours.

It pours
From
My heart
My flesh
Effervescing as
Tenderness

Feel free
To be
Secure
In me.

Be
Free
Totally free
Just
Love
Me
As
You
Do

It
Will
Come
Back
To you
Eternally.

© 1986

TOASTS FOR A GLOOMY AFTERNOON

Background

It's not usually the weather that makes us gloomy. The mail carrier's cry of "Neither rain or snow, nor sleet or hail will keep us from making our appointed rounds," attests to the underlying reality—that it's a motivation problem.

So, what really makes us gloomy? For us, it's when things don't go the way we want them to or expect them to. An unexpected business slowdown; a big bill that wasn't contemplated; goals not reached—on time. Fortunately, these are temporary situations—unless we allow them to fester.

Our approach to these little setbacks is to "have a toast." Toast them away—being careful, of course, not to overdo it. Remember, you must replace the loss with renewed commitment to keep your goals— your standards and to be thankful for how much you've attained at this point in your lives.

TOASTS FOR A GLOOMY AFTERNOON

Toast No. l.
"Whenever I am with you, the sun shines."

Toast No. 2.
"Your wonderful smile makes me smile."

Toast No. 3.
"Each day with you is spent in paradise."

Toast No. 4.
"There is no laughter without you."

Toast No. 5.
"A kiss from you makes the day worth living."

Toast No. 6.
"Sharing life with you is all that matters."

Toast No. 7.
"You are my sun shining through the rain."

Toast No. 8.
"Thank you for sharing this crazy adventure of
living with me."

Toast No. 9.
"I found my pot of gold when I found you."

Toast No. 10.
"Your love and laughter are the rainbow in my day."

LOVE FALLING MY WAY

Background

When does the fantasy start? A few words—a reply suggesting something of your personality—it's the slightest of things that brings two hearts together. This is a reflection back on our first meeting.

LOVE FALLING MY WAY

It was a sideways glance
Passing by my way.
It was just happenstance
I was looking that way.
Your face has been haunting
Me all day.

Can't work; can't eat!
Don't know what to say—
How to meet—
How to greet—
And ask you to stay.

It was a sideways glance
That became my trance;
That made my feelings dance.
I couldn't get away!
Your eyes have been teasing
Me all day.
Can't write; can't think!
Don't know what I'll say.
How to treat
Someone sweet—
Will she think it's play?

It was a sideways glance
That started romance
One surprising day.
I took a daring chance
Your love would fall my way
Everyday.

© 1991

ROMANTIC TOASTS TO CELEBRATE EVENTS

Background

I don't know if our lives are like most other people. We assume so. Sometimes I think the world is just one— emergency or disaster after another—If it isn't paying the mortgage, it's insurance, it's electricity, it's groceries, it's birthdays—it's just EVERYDAY!

There are those milestones that are worth remembering, and an evening out with a few toasts is a just commemoration of the occasion. We should have some special way of noting it on our time capsule, however.

What are the milestones? They will be different for all couples. For us, marriage was a very special event. Celebrating that once a year, however, would never do. We toast our good fortune in having the chance to share our lives together, everyday. We celebrate reaching new pinnacles! Buying that dream home—getting a new painting completed—getting better office space—paying off major bills—repaying friends who believed in us when it seemed like no one in their "right mind" should.

The traditional birthdays, wedding anniversaries, Valentines' Day, Fourth of July, Labor Day, Memorial Day, Grandparents' Day, Mother and Fathers' Days—and all the other DDAAAAAYYSSS—we celebrate for OTHERS. We save up! Then, we take a few days in retreat from the excitement of these events and spend bonding and loving time together— ALONE—sharing in the true joy of just being together.

ROMANTIC TOASTS TO CELEBRATE EVENTS

Toast No. 1.
"Thank you for making our home a show place!"

Toast No. 2.
"Thank you for being an incredible partner and for making our lives successful!"

Toast No. 3.
"Nothing is impossible with you, but without you, I'm afraid nothing will succeed."

Toast No. 4.
"Day and night in or out of sight—you are my total delight."

Toast No. 5.
"Living with you is an inspiration for life!"

Toast No. 6.
"Thank you for risking your life with me."

Toast No. 7.
"How can so much talent, truth, devotion and emotion be in YOU?—You are my great lady, beyond belief!"

Toast No. 8.
"You make the adventure of living fun."

Toast No. 9.
"Thank you for loving me."

Toast No. 10.
"I wish this night together would never end."

OUR LOVE IS MORE THAN TWO

Background

In the middle of the night, literally, these thoughts came word-for-word to my mind. I had been thinking of writing Gail another love poem for some months, but could not get the time. Our business had been particularly difficult—The Gulf War—had put everyone on the sidelines being a war quarterback instead of buying and selling homes. Everyone was frozen. No one could make decisions even though the market had extremely good opportunities. This period lasted for six months and crippled the country's economy. I was afraid that Americans were becoming locked in emotions and had lost the ability to think and act independently. We can't accomplish anything if we let the outer world's conditions take precedence over our own.

OUR LOVE IS MORE THAN TWO

Our Love is more than two.
It's true!

Our Love is more than two.
You give your love to me.
I give my love to you.

One plus one is two.
That's true.

But, you see, the love
You give to me
 Makes me more than me.
And the love I give to you
Makes you more than you.

So, you see,
Our love is more than two!
This is true.

It's no wonder, then,
That I should need
And love you more each day
When you add
More to me each day.

And so, my precious Love,
With you I will always stay.
And you
Will have to put up with me
From day to day
And day after day come what may.

For if there was ever a loss
Of you from me,
Then, less than me would be.

For all the Love you have given me
Has made me more than me
And subtracting that from me
Would now make me less than me
And even less than one.

And since
In human terms this cannot be
Our love, in consequence,
Must last through all eternity.

And it's your fault, you see
For making more of me
Than I ever thought could be.

© 1991

SPECIAL THOUGHTS

LOYALTY

Background

*M*arriage is a friendship. It requires ultimate faith and trust in one another. Your spouse should be your friend. No one will know you better. Their involvement in your life adds to achievement and self-fulfillment, just as your contribution to your spouse's life will do.

When Gail and I met, one of the things we were looking for was a true friend. We are fortunate. Our values, goals and outlook on life are very similar. We've had enough living experience to know our true natures and needs. We know enough to be ourselves so that our true feelings don't get submerged into just being "nice people." Our respect for one another's feelings is paramount. We try to be careful listeners for each other's points of view.

The poem "Loyalty" and Gail's painting of the same name was a combined creation. We tried to create complementary images. Hers, of course, is visual and mine is verbal. The painting and poem are available in print form.

"Loyalty" may not seem like a love poem, but its virtues and feelings are inseparable in the marriage relationship. When you stop being friends, you stop being lovers. Other problems follow. Keeping up a facade only lasts so long. The real fun of marriage is being friends.

This poem and painting are one of a series of twelve. The title to the series is "Twelve Women Whose Names End In The Sound of 'E'." It is a set of paintings and poems which attempt to depict a woman's life. We will be turning the set into a calendar. Several of the paintings and poems are available now.

LOYALTY

When someone
Believes in me
I beam with joy
See a brighter sun

Shining on my history.
Making the long haul
Of time and space
A joyful place.

A friend sharing
In my life
Lessens the strife
Makes celebrating

Life's little glories
Worthwhile stories.
Encourages achievement
Self-fulfillment.

Expands my vision
Making me willing
To tackle new horizons.
A friend sees me

For what I am,
Honestly.
A simple soul
Striving to be more.

Looking for opportunity's door
But, having frailty
And inconsistency;
Living imperfectly.

Their faith
Is sustaining
Even when problems
Seem overwhelming.

Encouraging me
And supporting me.
Renewing my strength
Pushing me on to victory.

Their loyalty
Makes me
Strive to be
A better me.

© 1987

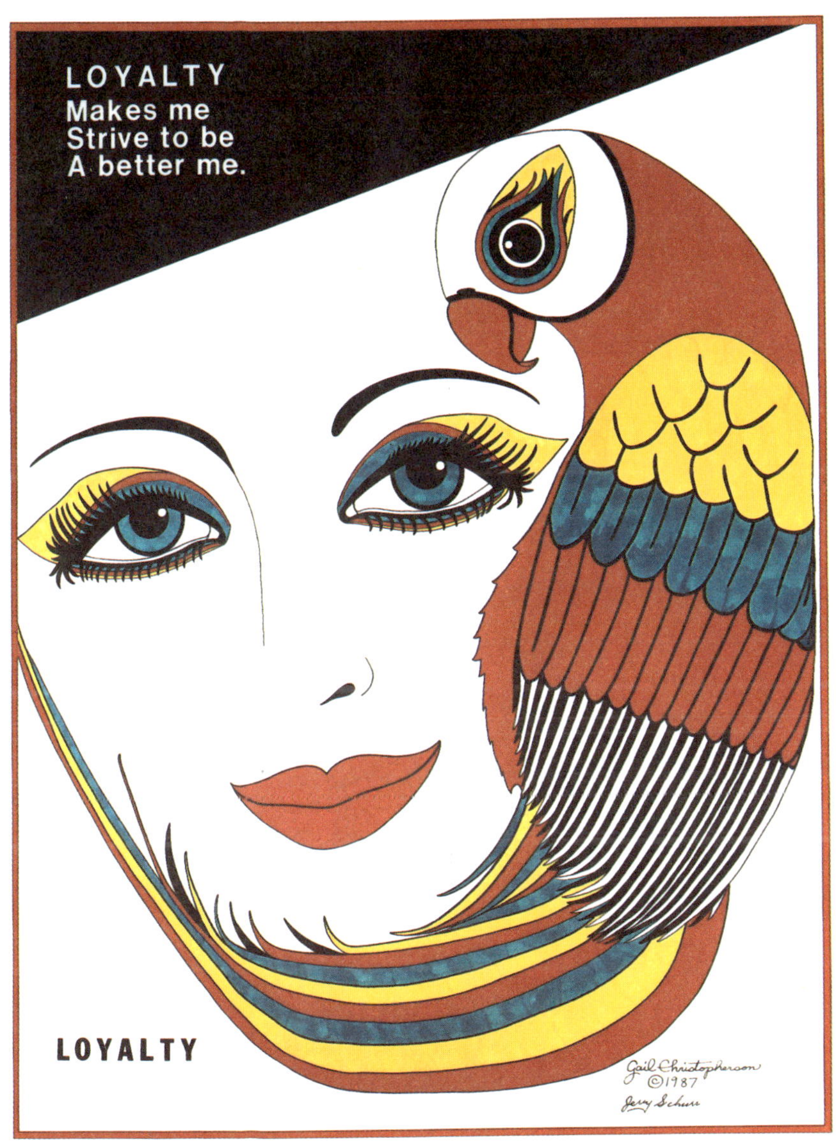
LOYALTY
Makes me
Strive to be
A better me.

LOYALTY

Gail Christopherson
©1987
Jerry Schurr

SPECIAL THOUGHTS

MARRY

Background

Marry is another poem from the series, "Twelve Women Whose Names End In The Sound Of 'E'." Gail thought that the poem should be included in this book because it really is a love poem. When I think about my own feelings regarding the wedding experience, the feelings are the same. I would have to change the he, him, etc. to she and her, etc., however.

There is so much excitement as the special day nears. Our emotions are seemingly out of control. Happiness and fear, joy and sorrow, expectancy and dismay are running through our minds at breakneck speed. Adrenaline is flowing and growing. Staying calm is difficult if not impossible.

Finally, the moment passes. Suddenly, all the joy and happiness fade and we're left with this thought, "What did I do?" Your confidence returns as the days pass by, and perhaps it's at this moment the poem, "Marry," reaffirms the many decisions you made in the previous days, weeks and months.

The "Joan Rivers" show on television has a marriage episode every year. This year one of the experts said, "The average wedding, today, costs $12,000 - $16,000." It takes my breath away. I shouldn't let Gail read this because ours cost only a few hundred dollars. If we would have had that kind of money available, we would have taken an extended honeymoon.

This is, if you remember, our second marriage. We are not caught up with friends' or society's mandates regarding a marriage ceremony. We were too concerned about whether or not we had found the right soul mate.

Sometimes the preparations and the ceremony can cloud our feelings. Our expectations become exaggerated. It always comes back to the relationship. How you feel about one another and how you work together—that's right, WORK ! And don't forget the FUN of working and being together.

It's WONDERFUL !

MARRY

Bright and light
Is the world
Within my sight
Shining, surrounding me.

My love is showing
My joy is flowing
My soul is soaring
Something wonderful
Is happening.

I'm shedding my singularity
Expanding my responsibility
Giving my intimacy
To someone
Who believes in me.

He enjoys my simplicity
Respects my individuality
Delights in my capability
Loving even my personality.

When he's around
His gentle sound
Surrounds
All my activity
Lifting me
Inspiring me
To be as much as I can be.

Trusting
In my honesty
Accepting me
Openly.

No testing
No expecting
No dominance
No subservience
Just his thankfulness
That God created me.

Joy of joys
He is to me
All love and laughter
Today and hereafter.

Just two souls together
With their virtues growing
Stride for stride
Arm in arm
A singularity
Of love for love
In life's joyful unity
Eternal harmony.

Bright and light
Is the world
Within my sight
Shining, surrounding me.

My love is showing
My joy is flowing
My soul is soaring
Something wonderful
Is happening.

© 1987

MARRY

My love is showing
My joy is flowing
My soul is soaring
Something wonderful
Is happening. . .

ROMANTIC BOUQUETS

Background

*A*s a young teenager I had always wondered what the connection was between women and flowers. My feelings were that somehow the tradition was started, and then retailers pushed the idea as a commercial enterprise and wanted to make us "men" feel GUILTY for not going along with it.

Women also preyed upon the idea. If "this man" really loved me, he would send me FLOWERS. "Flowers for every occasion (and lack of occasion) would be the best way (for starters) to show me that he really cared about me."

The truth is—from my experience, of course, it's very difficult to throw a bouquet of flowers away. They create excitement from their color, fragrance–and thought. Everyone who sees the bouquet asks, "Who sent them?" I've never known of a woman to put them in a closet to hide them. They won't even throw them away if they come from someone they dislike.

So, men, remember flowers bring joys (about you) for hours and days and days. They don't put on weight and they do create a very happy, emotional state.

During the early months of our engagement, I sent Gail flowers. She saved some of the messages which we will share with you. I was really surprised that they meant so much to her.

I haven't sent her flowers for a few years. It's because I buy cut flowers and make arrangements for her every week at home. I enjoy the opportunity to be creative and have discovered that it really adds a lot to our lives to have fresh flowers in the house. It lifts you up emotionally and reminds you that there is "someone special" in the universe operating in our lives. At this point in life I would prefer to "not ever" be without flowers.

I don't believe the things I've said to Gail are any different from what other people feel inside or have expressed to their special someone. Perhaps they will be of help to you.

ROMANTIC BOUQUET NOTES

Bouquet No. 1.
"Thank you for bringing my soul to life."

Bouquet No. 2.
"Thank you for making my life new."

Bouquet No. 3.
"Your love makes my life real."

Bouquet No. 4.
"Thank You! For being a pure soul; kind, generous and patient —a truly beautiful soul mate."

Bouquet No. 5.
"It's only fair that I try to return some of the joy you've given me."

Bouquet No. 6.
"For bringing back all the colors in life I couldn't see."

Bouquet No. 7.
"I love you more than flowers can say each and everyday."

Bouquet No. 8.
"I hope our lives will blossom together forever."

Bouquet No. 9.
"Just a little reminder that tonight's a special night."

Bouquet No. 10.
"You're the special love in my life."

SPECIAL THOUGHTS

LONGEVITY

Background

Normally, when people get married, it's during an upbeat time. You feel stable in your life. You're confident of your abilities. You feel your mate will contribute to these conditions, too.

I haven't talked to any grooms who have said, "You know, I got fired from my job, so I decided to get married; and that's how I met—the special someone." Or, "You know, that auto accident I had that laid me up so badly, I decided to marry the first woman I found who was a nurse."

I asked Gail to marry me because I ran out of things to talk about—of course, not !

Gail represented to me, a chance to find fulfillment in myself, fulfillment for her—and for us to obtain a better understanding about life. We have total support for each other. We work hard everyday to make a success of our lives together. There is no jealousy; only hope and faith that our endeavors day after day will bring us more time to do what we enjoy most—which is to create art and poetry together that will bring happiness to others.

We had no wealth except what we found in each other. The wealth we enjoy today could literally be wiped out tomorrow. But, the joy of loving that we share together can never be lost—that's why we have longevity.

LONGEVITY

How long will we be
Sharing in our ecstacy
Of holding hands and arms
And physical intimacy?

How long will we be
Sharing eyes and ears
And joys and tears
As we pursue our history?

How long will we be
Taking walks and talks
Searching and planning
And laughing about life's incredibility?

How long will we be
Sharing the changes in you and me
As time slowly reveals its path
And takes control of our destiny?

How long will we be
Holding to our singular course
Steadfast for what we believe will last
Sharing with others the joy that life should be?

How long will we be
If it were up to me
And I could master time and fate
And hold back all that time can take
And make you love me and only me.

If it were up to me
And only me
Then your life would have to be
Entwined with mine and only mine
And I with yours and only yours.

And you would have to take from me
The very best that I could be
For the very best that I can be
Is what I wish for you from me.
And with this wish no misery
Or hardships less than that of ecstacy.

For what I wish
If it were up to me
Is to be more than mortals be
To share life with you
Beyond eternity
To have life go on and on
Until our souls are song.

That is what I wish would be
If it were up to me.

© 1991

THE ARTIST AND THE AUTHOR
Gail Christopherson-Schurr and Jerry Schurr

SPECIAL THOUGHTS

ELEGANT LOVE

Background

This poem represents my experience with Gail as a busy mother, career woman and wife. It should be thought of as a tribute to Gail (and all mothers with children). The boy in the painting is our son, Todd. I have watched the busy nonstop schedules required by mothers for good parenting, housekeeping and family harmony. Few men could do it, and fewer still would ever attempt it unless there was no choice. This, then is my salute to "Motherhood," and the fabulous things you are able to do.

ELEGANT LOVE

Eyes round and peering
Look out from the ship they are steering
Swept along in Mother's song
Through life racing.

Looking her best
Passing the rest
Lives held together by embracing.

Eyes round and peering
Joyful life appearing
Dressed and caressed
Ready for life steering.

Mom's out promoting
Even though she's child toting.
Life can't be on hold
When time says, "Be bold!"

She's a mother in fashion
With so much to do
Goals to accomplish
For her and her child, too.

From place to place
You see each face.
One happy and wondering
What they'll see new;

The other smiling and graceful
Full of expectancy, too;
Knowing her accomplishments
Are for more than just two.

So into town and out of town
You see the "racingest" two.
Into small shops and tall towers
Through sunshine and waterfall showers.

Smiling and graceful; dressed up like new
Nothing can daunt this spirited—two
Uphill and downhill, across flatlands and hot sand
Through rain-made puddles—
With nothing but cuddles

And bundles of love;
Tireless efforts and goals worthy of
Sharing with children and stars up above.

Eyes round and peering
Lives full of meaning
Such is elegant love.

ELEGANT LOVE

FINAL THOUGHTS

A KISS–a moment in time to reflect on love. As you may have guessed, Gail and I have had many moments that we have shared together on this special subject.

You may wonder how I have used these poems and toasts. It all started harmlessly as a way to express my love to Gail. I read one aloud to her as she was preparing dinner. She was very moved, and it led to other wonderful expressions of appreciation for each other including the bedroom one.

Since then, I have, as you can tell by this book, written many thoughts to Gail. They are all true feelings from my soul to hers. She deserves and has earned so much more than my few words. I do so hope that I can give her more in the future.

But, that's the chance we take, isn't it. It's the true adventure of living that we're after—hoping, of course, that there will be other dividends. Dividends being a kiss, love, children, better incomes, a nicer home, more vacation time, more time to create and share in the larger world.

There can be no greater reward for me than to share my life with Gail. We are absolutely compatible—true soul mates. We wish the same experiences for you.

If you or your "special one" takes a few moments and reads one of these poems to the other, we believe they will open up your feelings as they did for us. We certainly hope so, anyway.

You must keep in mind, however, that after sharing one of these poems, it might lead to "A KISS!" THEN, WATCH OUT!

Our love to you,

Jerry and Gail